# ANGRY E-MAIL

# HOW TO PUT A LID ON IT

# ANGRY E-MAIL

# HOW TO PUT A LID ON IT

Dona J. Young

*Angry E-Mail:*
*How to Put a Lid on It*

By Dona J. Young
May 29, 2011
Copyright © Writer's Toolkit Publishing LLC

Cover design by Nanc Ashby
SavelDesign.com

ISBN-13: 978-1463545895
ISBN-10: 1463545894
Library of Congress Control Number  2011910511

Writer's Toolkit Publishing LLC
www.wtkpublishing.com

Printed in the United States.
This book is printed on acid-free paper.

To Reggie

# Contents

# Introduction

Technology can lead even smart people in top-level positions to lose touch with the human element of communication. When that happens, e-mail can be used in a dehumanizing way and, at times, turn into front-page news.

In August 2006, Radio Shack created a storm of attention by sending out an e-mail telling 400 employees that their jobs were over. The company defended itself by stating that the employees who received the message had all been informed that they would be notified electronically.

Though the message may have been carefully crafted and sent without malice, the seemingly heartless, yet super efficient way that e-mail was used added insult to injury. Another example comes from Great Britain. In February 2011, an army major sent a message to 38 long-standing soldiers that their jobs were being cut because of a reduced budget; one of the soldiers was on the front line in Afghanistan when he received the message.

How would you feel if all of your e-mail suddenly became public? When used in litigation, e-mail can become part of the public domain, which is what the former employees of Enron found out after the fact.

Every angry e-mail has two sides: sending and receiving. In fact, you may find it easier to deal with an angry e-mail that you receive than to keep yourself from sending one. Stress can cause momentary lapses of judgment, and a computer screen can seduce a writer into composing a dramatic monologue.

Without a doubt, an angry e-mail can ruin a day or even side-track a career. As well, companies lose clients who feel offended by messages they receive or *don't* receive. Though experience is the best teacher, this book offers solutions for averting angry e-mail as well as for responding to them. By knowing the facts and following best practices, you can save yourself major headaches.

*Angry E-Mail* shows you how to use communication as a tool to enhance business relationships. You see, it's your relationships that support you in getting your job done—not simply the exchange of information through messages.

# Part 1

## Communication Is a *Process*, Not an Event

When professionals receive an angry e-mail, they are often taken by surprise. That's partly because e-mail has become the "go to" communication channel, even when e-mail is not the appropriate medium. For example, do you ever:

- Hide behind e-mail to avoid personal contact?
- Send long and complicated messages?
- Use e-mail to argue a point?
- Send bad news via e-mail?

If you answered *yes* to any of the above, you may be expecting too much from e-mail. When e-mail is used beyond its limits, one result is *information overload*. When messages are too long, readers may disconnect and save the e-mail for "later," which means no response is sent, essentially transferring frustration from the receiver to the sender.

When conveying bad news, e-mail may not even be a viable option; meeting in person is the preferred method to give bad news, especially when the news relates to something personal. However, when you must convey bad news in a message, use an indirect style.

Communication is not a one-sided broadcast; instead, to be effective, communication involves an exchange. However, a computer screen lulls writers into focusing so intently on their message that they lose sight of the fact that their message is meaningless unless they reach their reader.

With e-mail, writers not only get lost in their own ideas, feelings, and assumptions but also have few external controls to keep them from sending their messages. Flaming e-mail go out with the click of a button, leaving the writer's hands for good and, at times, creating serious and long-lasting issues.

Deb, a busy social worker from Chicago, said that whenever she felt the urge to express strong feelings in a message, her mantra would become, "Say it, forget it. Write it regret it."

By tuning in to readers' needs and expectations, you will use e-mail as a more flexible tool that achieves more effective results. By the focusing on the relationship, you put information in its rightful place in the exchange.

Let's explore how to deal with angry messages by putting communication in context and reviewing key principles for using e-mail effectively.


## Communicate to Enhance Business Relationships

A mission of all business communication, including e-mail, is building relationships based on trust.

The job gets done, in part, based on the quality of the relationships among the players. When people trust and respect each other, they cooperate and a synergy develops. When people do not respect each other, a project becomes problematic: people engage in power plays and withhold information. Add the ineffective use of e-mail to that mix, and the human element gets further discounted.

According to John, an academic director, technology can easily stifle the human element and control the direction that communication takes. John shared that whenever he received an e-mail that asked *how and why* something happened, his response was simple: "When can we meet—I'd rather talk about it."

A written response can turn an already dysfunctional situation into e-mail war: technology has severe short-comings compared to live human interaction that includes subtleties that cannot even be described in words. However, professionals consistently let the ease and efficiency of e-communication seduce them into using e-mail, even when tensions run high.

At every juncture, *effective* communication relies on decisions that lead to enhanced trust and respect. One key is to keep the human element alive in communication. Another key is understanding that people are more important than projects. When things don't feel right, it's time to stop and think rather than rely on the most convenient option.

Ask yourself, whose projects do you make a priority? Is it the colleague who shows you kindness and respect, or the one who treats you like a corporate robot?

## Understand Both Sides of Tone

Tone is a two-way street: how a *reader interprets* a message and how a *writer conveys* it. For instance, when you receive a message, if you infer a problem, you may respond in such a manner so that you actually create one.

For example, when Rose received an abrupt message from her client Bob saying that he had to cancel an important meeting, she didn't know how to respond. Rose was already having a bad day and assumed that Bob was no longer interested in speaking with her. Rather than give in to her feelings of rejection, Rose wrote back that she understood and thanked him for the heads up.

This time, when Bob wrote back, he apologized for cancelling, saying that he was under pressure getting ready for an unexpected audit and that he was looking forward to meeting with her as soon as it was over.

Business communication occurs in context, and the players create the context as they go along. The last interaction tends to set the tone for the current status of the relationship—that's why one angry e-mail can have such a disastrous outcome. Whenever you read a message that you think sounds angry, ask yourself, "Am I interpreting this correctly?"

Understanding comes in layers, and the first reading of anything does not necessarily provide the correct understanding. By putting a message aside for an hour or a day, your feelings will change because you will have gotten past the initial knee-jerk reaction that the message would have triggered.

By keeping an open mind, you can take a proactive approach to find out information to clarify the situation, relieving nagging doubts and fears.

## Develop a Strategy, Not Simply a Response

When an angry e-mail seems to be pointed at you personally, the most important thing that you can do is press the *pause* button before you send your response. Developing a strategy is that *pause* button: by putting the message in context, you give yourself a chance to develop a response based on well-thought-out choices rather than your feelings in the moment.

Feelings are contagious, especially negative ones such as anger and frustration. In addition, feelings are in constant flux—you will feel differently and have more perspective by putting distance between the first reading and your response.

In the meantime, get in touch with your feelings and the motives attached to them: Are you feeling like a victim pointing blame on someone else? Or are you feeling like a villain trying to inflict pain, wanting someone to pay? Neither of these motives will result in anything productive.

By identifying your feelings and motivations, you are able to gain insight that allows you to separate your feelings from the issue. The objectivity that results allows you to expand your perspective to find common ground; areas of agreement have a bonding effect.

- First, put the communication in context by asking:
  What are my objectives? What do I hope to achieve?
  What is our common ground or mission?
  What do we agree about?

- Next, develop two potential responses and compare them:
  What are the risks and benefits of each?
  How will each response affect the feelings of those involved?
  Will the response help solve the problem or escalate it?
  What is the potential outcome of each?

- In addition to broad questions, consider specific issues:
  How does the power structure affect your thinking?
  Should you *reply all*? Are you inclined to *reply all* simply because you think that you should?
  Are you in some way responsible for the situation?
  Would an apology be in order?
  What outcome would you prefer?
  What time frame is involved?

Venting is good for the soul. As an ancient saying tells us, "If you let it out, it will free you; if you hold it in, it will destroy you." Pay careful attention, however, when you "let it out." E-communication is never the appropriate outlet.

In fact, the only appropriate outlet is a private one: journal or talk with a friend, therapist, or coach. Write your draft, but do not edit it until you feel clear-headed, objective, and confident. Leave it for a while and then do another edit before sending.

Angry messages impress no one. Each person who reads an angry message realizes that he or she could be the next target. You see, an angry e-mail is less about the situation and more about the way the situation is being handled.

Therefore, avoid doing anything compulsively: take the time that you need, realizing that a hasty response can have negative and long-lasting consequences. Thus, even if you think people are eagerly awaiting your response, focus on *your* needs—what do you need so that you can develop an effective response? Information, time, understanding, clarity, or maybe a good night's sleep?

If the writer poses no questions, consider if you need to respond at all. When you respond to someone who you feel has attacked you, be careful not to add credibility to the attack. Defending yourself will only make you sound . . . well, *defensive*. In addition, do not feel obliged to *reply all*; by keeping the communication between yourself and the sender, you maintain more control and dignity.

Though you may not feel like speaking to the other person, consider if making a phone call would lead to a better solution. Depending on the power structure and who sent the message, you may consider "phoning a friend" for advice. Make it your goal to achieve more than simply responding to the problem at hand; also find a way to support the broader mission. When someone takes the lead in harmonizing a relationship, others notice.

The world is moving at warp speed, and everyone involved has other immediate concerns. Just because you are dwelling on this situation does not mean that anyone else is, including the sender. You see, the author of the angry e-mail felt differently as soon as he or she clicked *send*.

As soon as someone sends an angry e-mail, that person experiences a sense of relief but also possibly a sense of guilt, grief, and remorse. That's because insight often comes after the fact, which is a painful way to learn a lesson. An angry e-mail puts both the sender and the receiver in a vulnerable position.

Craft your message in tune with your communication strategy—solve the bigger problem, if there is one. Measure your best solution by whether it will work toward enhancing trust and thus the business relationship. It's not about becoming someone's BFF; it's about staying focused on getting the job done effectively.

## Nurture Trust: Give the *Benefit of the Doubt*

Trust takes time to develop and can be fragile. To give someone the benefit of the doubt is to believe something good about the person rather than something bad when both are possibilities.

When you assume someone is intentionally trying to cause you harm, you are setting yourself up for a *fight or flight* response. When you need to defend yourself (from a real or an imagined threat), you tap into automatic response patterns over which you do not have conscious control. Whenever you can assume that slights were unintentional, you are doing yourself a favor.

Assume that the situation is not about you personally; separate yourself from the issue at hand. Use your soft skills—your people skills—to open the exchange of ideas; clients need to feel as if they are being listened to.

However, those times when you can't let go of negative feelings, clarify the issue before you even start to develop your response.

- Could you be transferring the emotions from some other unresolved issue to this situation?

- Have you experienced a loss that you could still be grieving?

You see, anger is a stage of the grieving process. When people experience loss, they are often unaware that unresolved feelings are waiting to be triggered in the form of anger. Anger related to grief is difficult to identify and difficult to control once it is triggered.

When you feel especially angry or receive what you believe is someone else's anger, remember the sage and ancient advice given by Philo of Alexandria, "Be kind, for everyone is fighting a great battle."

Clearly more factors are at play than the words used to convey the message. So let's take a look at some factors that are not apparent on the surface.

## Listen to Micro-Messages: What Makes People Mad?

Micro-messages are the unspoken messages *between the lines*. Everything that you say and *don't say* sends a message.

For example, perhaps you write to someone asking an important question, but days pass and you still don't receive a response. What micro-message are you receiving? How does it make you feel?

You have no way of knowing why someone does not respond, but you do know how their lack of response makes you feel. The offender, in fact, is sending a negative micro-message of which he or she may not even be aware.

Since communication occurs in cycles, unanswered questions leave a situation ripe for misinterpretation. The longer someone waits for an important response, the more likely other factors enter the dialogue. That's because people feel disrespected when they do not receive an anticipated response; the relationship suffers and some trust is lost.

Getting no response or being ignored is only one reason why people can become angry, here are some others:

- Being told bad news in an abrupt manner
- Being told "No, I can't help you" or "That's our policy"
- Not seeing promised results
- Feeling disrespected, accused, or threatened
- Being blamed or shamed
- Working hard to understand a message
- Working hard to respond to a complicated message
- Knowing someone has read a request and still not responded
- Being drilled on an issue when analysis is inappropriate
- Receiving an angry message: feelings are contagious

People also feel slighted for unpredictable reasons; even so, you can improve communication by *managing expectations* effectively. For example, should you say that you will do something but then do not follow through, the person on the other end is going to feel disappointed.

Some people put off responding because they have difficulty understanding what the writer needs. Long, unclear, complicated messages make the reader work hard to respond, and no one likes to work harder than needed.

The easier you can make it for the reader to respond, the better. For example, when you pose more than one question, number them. Numbering is a form of visual persuasion that aids the reader in understanding your message at a glance.

At times, people write angry e-mail because they feel stress from personal issues such as illness, family concerns, and economics difficulties. At those times, a little compassion and understanding go a long way.

At other times, a writer will use angry e-mail to try to sway a decision: an angry e-mail rarely changes a decision. In fact, the other parties are more likely to respond by digging their heals deeper into their position. Regardless of the circumstances, an angry e-mail causes its writer to lose both credibility and trust.

*Here's the bottom line*: Though you cannot control how others will respond, you can learn more about your reader. The more you know, the more equipped you are to manage your expectations and communicate in tune with another's style.

**Understand Your Client's Worldview:**

## R E S P E C T  Diversity

The Golden Rule states, "Do unto others as you would have them do unto you." However, when people have diverse backgrounds, the Platinum Rule trumps the Golden Rule. The Platinum Rule states, "Do unto others as *they* would have you do unto *them*."

To illustrate, have you ever given someone a gift that you loved and would wish to receive yourself, but the recipient did not value it the way that you did? Consider the Platinum Rule as you gain insight into *personal*, *cultural*, and *generational* expectations.

For example, shortly after the Madoff scandal broke, retired teacher Arlene sent an e-mail to her broker asking how much money was in her account. Her broker Sam was barraged with calls and e-mail, many of which sounded urgent, which Arlene's message did not. Sam also knew that all monthly statements had just been sent out. As a result, Sam didn't make responding to Arlene a priority; and after a day or two, he forgot to respond. Several days later, Sam was shocked to receive papers from Arlene transferring her account to another broker.

Sam's assumption was that Arlene needed information that was already on its way to her; however, Arlene wanted to make sure that her money was safe. As a Boomer, Arlene diligently followed a professional protocol her entire career, and she expected everyone else to follow the same protocol.

Because Arlene was ready to retire, this issue was critically important to her; she felt insulted when she did not receive a reply. Instead of saying what was on her mind, she sent a stronger message.

*Generational Diversity:* What is your generation's *style*?

Have you noticed that each generation communicates in its own unique style? Are you aware of how to work with people of different generations to develop trust and respect?

Though sources vary, here's a rough breakdown of the various generations:

- Veterans and Silent Generation, born 1925 to 1945
- Baby Boomers, born 1945 to 1964
- Generation X, born 1964 to 1980
- Generation Y or Millenniums, born 1980 to 2000

One major difference in the way that different generations communicate is their use of e-communication; though many Veterans and Boomers use e-mail effectively, many still prefer phone calls and face-to-face communication.

Veterans and Boomers are known for *not saying* what is on their minds, but instead *they tend to make people guess.* Veterans and Boomers grew up in eras in which politeness and protocol kept communications running smoothly. In fact, many base their decisions on protocol, not necessarily how they feel in the moment: Veterans, and Boomers to a lesser extent, were taught that their feelings were not relevant when it comes to business, but getting the job done was.

In fact, many professional Boomers gave up personal lives so that they could be successful in their professional careers. In contrast, younger generations expect to have both: a successful personal life and a successful career. Boomers do not always understand when younger generations are not willing to make the same sacrifices.

If a personal problem arises with a Veteran or Boomer, take it seriously and deal with it proactively: most of the time you can melt the problem by showing some attention to the issue and respect to the person. When a Boomer acts suspiciously, often the real the message the Boomer is trying to send is "Respect me, and I'll be nice."

*Gen Xers* prefer e-mail and instant messages. In contrast to Boomers, Gen Xers do not make you guess, *they tell it like it is*. Listen to what they have to say and stay connected. Once they speak their minds, you and the Gen Xers should both move on.

Gen Xers are technically savvy, and they use technology to stay connected with friends and family. Gen Xers also play an important role: they provide a bridge between Boomers and Nexters, buffering communication so that misunderstandings are averted.

*Nexters* prefer text messaging, instant messaging, and blogging. Nexters are unique in that *they ask for what they want*. They sound more confident than older generations in the way that they communicate. Though Nexters do not make you guess or wait for you to ask them what is going on; when they do speak up, older generations can interpret Nexters as being disrespectful and abrupt.

On the job, Nexters expect the newest technology, and they use it constantly to stay connected with friends and family. When Nexters ask for information, they are more interested in getting their answer quickly than in being treated politely. In contrast, when a Boomer makes a request, the Boomer expects to be treated with respect. If a Veteran's requests are ignored or treated abruptly, expect a reaction, which may come in the form of passive-aggressive behavior.

Communication is like a dance, and each generation dances differently, resulting in a slightly different tone. Know your client's style and respect it—how people communicate contributes to who they are as human beings. Also, by not reading too much into the meaning behind the style, you will encounter fewer obstacles.

When you do encounter obstacles, mirror your client's behavior and style. Mirroring amplifies similarities: similarities enhance relationships while differences help create a wedge.

*Personal Diversity*: Are you a *thinker* or a *feeler*?

Along the wide spectrum of ways that personalities differ is the *thinker-feeler* category. The Meyers-Briggs Type Indicator (MBTI) scores that difference: If you score high on either *thinking* or *feeling*, your writing style will reflect your personality type.

- *Thinkers* tend to get right to the point and make little or no effort to connect with the reader as one human to another.

- *Feelers* tend to overemphasize connecting with their readers.

While thinkers tend to sound abrupt, feelers tend to include fluff in their writing. The key is to find balance.

Review the three messages that follow, starting with the balanced message and then comparing how a thinker or a feeler might respond.

### *Balanced* message:

Hi Mitchell,

Will you be going to the upcoming training in D.C.? If so, would you have time to meet with me to discuss the new program we are offering this fall?

Hope your day is going well.

Helen

### *Extreme Thinker* response:

I'm not going to D.C.

### *Extreme Feeler* response:

Hi Helen,

How are you doing? Thanks for checking in with me about the D.C. training. I'm sorry to say that I won't be attending the training, so we'll have to figure something else out about discussing the new program offering. Sorry about that. I hope you have a great time in D.C. and will miss seeing you there.

Hope you have a great day. Thanks again.

Mitchell

Each extreme has its own drawback: the key is balance. A balanced approach is easy to achieve with minimum effort: thinkers need to add a human touch by using salutations and closings and even niceties once in a while; feelers need to take out some of the "extra stuff" in their messages, often referred to as *fluff*.

Thinkers and feelers can both benefit from examining how they use *thank you*: thinkers sometimes overlook saying *thank you* while feelers tend to say it automatically and too often. Say *thank you* only once in a message and only in response to someone giving you assistance. And by the way, *thank you* is more effective than "thank you in advance," even if the deed is yet to be done.

To find more balance, first accept diversity in other people's communication styles; in other words, stop judging another's style. Next, adjust your own style so that it is more balanced.

*Cultural Diversity:* Do you use a *direct* or an *indirect style*?

Cultures differ in important ways, and one dimension is *context,* the unspoken cultural norms and rituals. To start, think of a culture as being either *low context* or *high context*.

In *low context* cultures:

- People interact with few rituals—communication is somewhat informal and not very structured.
- People use a **direct style** to communicate: the *words* are more important than the situation.

In *high context* cultures:

- People follow shared protocol which defines how they will interact. Communication is more structured and more formal.
- People use an **indirect style** to communicate: the situation helps define the encounter; thus, the words alone may not convey the meaning of the communication.

People from low context cultures, such as the U.S., tend to use a *direct style* of communication. People who use a direct style get right to the point and can feel comfortable speaking in a highly personal way, even with strangers. In business environments, direct communicators get down to business quickly, dismissing small talk until they finish the deal.

In contrast, people from high context cultures use an *indirect style* and generally communicate in an impersonal way at first; anything too personal can be highly offensive. For example, people from high context cultures, such as Japan, South America, India, and some parts of Europe, prefer to follow formal protocol, especially in the beginning. Getting down to business too quickly can put off people from high context cultures. Indirect communicators include a lot of small talk until they develop trust and respect, then they are ready to do business.

In fact, even in the U.S., various segments of the country differ in their communication styles. Northerners tend to be more direct than Southerners, and people from the Northeast tend to be more direct than people from the Midwest.

Indirect communicators can mistake direct communi-cation as being rude; in contrast, direct communicators can be impatient with indirect communication. When people communicate using diverse styles, the situation is ripe for misassumptions.

For example, Bill, a highly successful financial analyst from Dallas said, "When I'm up North, people seem to assume I'm not as smart as I am because I tend to be quiet and keep my opinions to myself. I don't speak up in meetings until I have something important to say, and sometimes people react surprised by my comments."

People who communicate indirectly place a high value on being polite, and asking questions directly sometimes feels rude. For example, indirect communicators may exchange two or three messages before actually stating their question, making their request or saying exactly what they mean. Direct communicators, on the other hand, can become frustrated with this type of back and forth "banter."

**Direct Communicator:**
Please give me one or two times next week that you are available for a phone meeting.

**Indirect Communicator:**
What is your availability for a call next week?

**Direct Communicator:**
I don't agree.

**Indirect Communicator:**
May I make a suggestion?

Though communication has more to do with a personal style than with geographical location; when someone is stereotyped because his or her communication style is different, everyone loses.

To adapt to cultural diversity, neither judge nor be easily offended. Be patient and give the other person the benefit of the doubt. In fact, the best solution in diverse environments is *authenticity*: sincerity, humility, and consideration.

## Apologize Gracefully

Apologies help diffuse highly-charged emotions. An apology is less about admitting a mistake than it is about reassuring a client that you take a situation seriously and are eager to resolve the issue.

The worst approach to take is a stance of "I'm right and you're wrong." All situations include shades of grey—no one is ever all right or all wrong. The sooner you can claim accountability for the part that you play, the sooner the other side can become open to listening.

When a situation calls for an apology, dissolve hurt feelings by apologizing quickly and humbly. Don't use excuses. As Henry David Thoreau once advised, "One cannot too soon forget his errors and misdemeanors; for to dwell on them is to add to the offense."

**Don't say:**
I'm really sorry that I couldn't get back to you sooner, but I had several other projects that needed urgent attention. Your message was on my priority list, but I couldn't get to it until now.

**Do Say:**
I apologize for not getting back to you sooner; thank you for being patient. What can I do now to assist you?

**Do Say:**
I'm sorry that I could not get back to you sooner. I appreciate your patience as well as the opportunity to work with you on this project. Attached are the papers you requested.

Keep your apology simple, and also take the opportunity to reinforce the relationship by showing appreciation.

If you feel emotional, your words will convey your feelings as well as your ideas. When someone writes you with emotion, try to understand what provoked the person's actions; then wait until you gain a clear perspective *before* you respond.

*Before being defensive, ask yourself:*

How can I apologize without sounding accusatory or self-deprecating?

**Don't say:**

I'm sorry that this got botched up again; I was really trying to get this done on time, but three people called in sick, and I was the only one handling all of our accounts. Hope you understand.

**Do Say:**

I apologize for the delay—we were short staffed. I appreciate working with you and have developed additional controls so that this does not happen again.

*Before going on the offensive, consider the following:*

Could something serious be going on, such as illness, death of a loved one, or a stressful economic situation?

**Don't say:**

I sent you a message yesterday and have yet to receive a response. I know you have instant access to your messages, so can you please take the time to answer my question!

**Do Say:**

I'm just following up on my request from the other day. Will you be able to help me by Friday? That's when my report is due.

An appropriate wait time for receiving a response is two days, so try to wait that long before following up about a lack of response. However, if you receive one of the previous messages, respond quickly.

**Don't say:**

I couldn't figure out what you were asking, so I put your message aside until I had more time and didn't get back to it. Sorry.

**Do say:**

Sorry about the delay. I'll work on your request immediately—can you clarify which numbers you need for your report?

When a message strikes you the wrong way, do not put anything in writing until you clarify your understanding.

When you feel good about yourself, you are likely to deal well with any kind of challenge that comes your way. In contrast, when you feel as if the world is beating up on you, you may act defensive or even go on the offensive, reaping unpleasant results. Make important decisions only when you feel confident and objective.

## Delay Sending Messages

Often a writer gains insight into a better solution as soon as he or she clicks *send*; with e-mail, insight after the fact can be painful.

*When in doubt, do not send a message out.* Save your message in **Drafts** until the next day. Whenever you feel intense emotions as you compose, delete the recipient's name after "To" in the heading.

Cynthia, an insightful human resource manager, said that at times she puts in her own name as the recipient. When she receives and reads the message later, she is sometimes shocked by her tone, which seemed so neutral as she was composing it.

In fact, you can adjust your settings so that even after you click **Send,** your messages can be held in your **Outbox** for a specified time. To set your controls for this additional safeguard, go to your **Inbox** and search "delay send messages." Whatever you do, do not act impulsively.

One executive shared that he used the delay option on all of the messages he sent, even routine messages. The delay option allowed him to go back into a message to clarify a point instead of sending a second message later, saving time in the long run.

Once again, communication is a process, and understanding comes in layers. For the best results, embrace the process.

### Call, Don't Write

The key to communication is the relationship, not the information. Therefore, when you find yourself hiding behind e-mail to avoid someone, call or set up a meeting. A human voice can melt fears and negative feelings in a way that e-mail cannot.

When communication feels complicated, something below the surface is going on. It's easy to react to fears and negativity with avoidance; however, by continuing to cooperate and be supportive, you show your flexibility and strength.

By placing your focus on building trust and respect, you are nurturing the relationship. In the process, you are also enhancing your own emotional intelligence.

### Manage Expectations

Expectations come in two forms: the *spoken* and the *unspoken*. Expectations are also perceptions. You help your clients manage their expectations when you assist them in perceiving a situation realistically and in tune with what you can and cannot provide.

Clarify perceptions, spoken and unspoken, to the extent possible. The only way to ensure that everyone shares a common understanding is to put it in writing: writing keeps everyone on the same page, so to speak. To stay in sync, provide written updates.

One way to improve perceptions is to build in reasonable "wiggle room" for deadlines and costs—going over budget never settles well, but going under budget always does.

Develop two due dates for projects: an external due date that you are positive that you can meet and an internal deadline that arrives sooner. When you can deliver sooner, you will have exceeded your client's expectations—as compared to cutting yourself short and then not meeting expectations.

People who try their best at times cut themselves short, taking care of others at the expense of not taking care of their own needs. The often-told story about oxygen on an airplane applies here: When told to put on oxygen masks, whose mask should you put on first, your own or your child's?

By putting your oxygen mask on first, you will have the breath to put your child's mask on too. The same is true in business. When you are working on a project, you are the only one who can plan your day. If you are always cutting yourself to the bare minimum, you are setting yourself up to fail; or at best, to meet expectations but not to exceed them.

At those times when you cannot meet a client's expecta-tions, communicate early, apologize, and give them a perk to add value, if that's possible.

Ask for what you want—don't wait for someone to read your mind, or you are setting yourself up to be angry. In addition, communicate in an honest way: though the adage, "It's easier to ask for forgiveness than to ask for permission," may be true, that approach strains relationships because it violates trust.

## Accept Instead of Expect

According to Italian psychiatrist Alessandro Ferretti, "The most difficult thing in life is to accept."

Life is about losses and compromises. No one leads a perfect life, and some losses are more painful to accept than others. In her book *Necessary Losses*, Judith Viorst eloquently describes the kinds of "illusions, dependencies, and impossible expectations that all of us have to give up to grow."[1]

One way to dissolve unrealistic expectations is to become more accepting. You may find that by being more accepting of yourself that you are able to be more accepting of others. No one is perfect—everyone makes mistakes. Adding forgiveness to the mix when needed changes the chemistry of a situation.

By managing your expectations effectively, you are likely to have an easier time managing your feelings as well as your actions.

Though controlling what others feel, say, or do is not an option, you can avert some issues by helping others manage their expectations of what you can and cannot do for them.

### End Note

1. Judith Viorst, *Necessary Losses*, Fireside, New York, 1998.

# Part 2

## What's the Point?

Communication flows effectively when a client can read a message, respond, and then move on. When a client struggles to understand what the writer needs or expects, communication becomes bogged down.

If you routinely write messages that are longer than one screen in length, you may want to reframe your understanding of the purpose of e-mail. In general, writing falls in one of the following four broad categories: *inform*, *create*, *persuade*, or *argue*.

For daily e-mail exchanges, if you find yourself doing any type of writing other than to *inform*, you may using e-mail beyond its limits. For example, persuasion is a complicated *process*; and if you find yourself using e-mail to try to convince someone about a point, you have chosen the wrong mode of communication.

The same is true with argument—arguing a point in an e-mail does not work. If a problem exists, e-mail is more likely to escalate the problem than solve it.

Communication involves more than words, and written communication lacks two significant elements—tone of voice and nonverbal behavior. Though communication is also more of an art than a science, some insight can be gained through research.

Albert Mehrabian showed that non-verbal elements are particularly important to communicate feelings and attitude.

In fact, at times, vocal and visual elements can contribute more to meaning than spoken words. Mehrabian concluded that, *when emotions are involved*, only 7 percent of meaning comes from words, with 38 percent coming from tone, and 55 percent from body language. Thus, Mehrabian's 7-38-55 rule.[1]

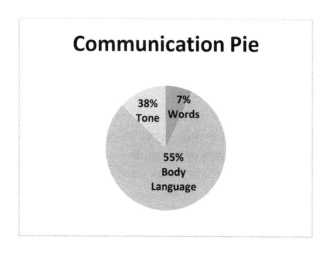

How does that apply to e-mail? According to communication professor Lisa Greco, "When you have only words, words can become a 'sword.'"

Words can trigger emotions, leaving the reader to interpret meaning without the support of the other two vital elements of communication. Words alone, without human contact, leave communication open for misinterpretation.

Interpretation and projection go hand in hand, making it far too easy to read too much into what a writer is trying to say. Once emotional triggers are activated, they often result in further miscommunication.

The next time that you feel confused about why e-mail presents so many challenges, remember the human elements that it lacks.

## Think of E-Mail as a Sound Bite, Not a Movie Script

Effective messages are short, conveying manageable pieces of information.

When a writer covers a lot of information in one message, the entire message is often discounted. If you want to make it easy for your reader to respond, keep your message short—about one screen in length. When your communication gets complicated, phone your client instead of sending a message (or in addition to sending a message) so that you can discuss intricate points or explain them in a voicemail.

Also consider putting the details in an attachment, using a cover message to summarize and give brief instructions. As a wise writer once said, "This would be shorter if I had more time."

## Create a Personal Link with Your Reader

Use your client's name in the salutation, and finish your message by using a short closing. By adding a personal touch, you help keep the human element in communication alive.

Any number of closings are effective: *best regards*, *all the best*, or even a short phrase such as *have a great day* adds a human touch. Letting readers know, "I look forward to hearing from you" helps break down some of the communication fears and barriers and reminds your reader that you are a person who cares.

In fact, even if you have an automatic sign-off, consider typing your name at the end of your message. Though redundant, your name reinforces a personal link between you and the reader.

## Use Visual Persuasion

Persuasion involves understanding. Visual persuasion is the application of formatting tools and techniques to shape your message so that your reader can glean your key points at a glance.

For example, you enhance the readability of a message by numbering questions, using boldface font to stress words or dates, adding white space between parts, and using side headings.

However, fancy fonts and nontraditional colors are not effective tools to enhance your message; in fact, they detract from your credibility. Therefore, do not use ALL CAPs to make words stand out because to some people all caps connote shouting. Also, do not use all lower case unless you are a techie writing to another techie; but shift back to a traditional style when your audience changes.

Standard rules for grammar, punctuation, and capitalization apply to e-mail. Therefore, never use text-messaging abbreviations such as "i" or "ur" in an e-mail at work; when text language "slips through," your message loses credibility. (And you never know when a message will be forwarded or to whom.)

Use traditional non-serif fonts such as Arial or Calibri, size 10 or 11. Stay with conservative colors such as black or blue, and refrain from using emoticons. However, if you know your reader is visually impaired, increase the font size and use bold print.

Visual persuasion is one more way to serve your client, saving time for a busy professional who is barraged with reading and decision making. For details and examples, see *Eleven Steps to Instantly Improve Your Writing* or *A Guide for Business Writing*.[2]

## Make Key Points Instantly Visible

When you edit your message, ask these questions so that you can make your purpose directly accessible for your readers:

- What is the most important issue?
- What are my outcomes and conclusions?
- What action do I want the reader to take?

Readers want to know the outcome, not "how come." They want to know the end point, not all the points leading up to it. Most important, they want to know what you need from them so that they can respond.

However, writers often expend so much effort getting their ideas down that they get lost in their own detail. As a result, they do not step back to identify the difference between information that is important from information that is not important (and even irritating) to the reader.

When you edit, move your *key point* so that it is the *first point* of your message. Then analyze the detail. Though that detail led you to your insights and conclusions, that same detail is counterproductive for your readers. As Mark Twain once advised, "The more you explain it, the more I don't understand it."

The only time that you wouldn't get right to the point is when you are sharing bad news; a bad news message needs detail up front so that the reader can understand the rationale before hearing the bad news. (You will read more on bad news messages in Part 3: "What about Tone?")

## Include Action Needed in the Subject Line

Readers use subject lines to file their messages so they can refer back to them for details.

By using subject lines that reflect the content of your message, you show courtesy for your reader. Therefore, start with an accurate and descriptive subject line, but also adjust your subject line as you go back and forth about a topic, making decisions and shifting into new topics.

Because some professionals file their messages on the basis of subject lines, keep first words of subject lines the same, adding new information as the conversation evolves. For example, the subject "April Training Date" could change to "April 26 Training" once a date is set. Revised subject lines save the reader from opening numerous messages to find a date or a decision.

The most important information a reader needs from you is the action he or she must take. By putting a due date or action needed in the subject line, the reader knows at a glance what is expected. For example, here are some subject lines that assist a reader in understanding action needed:

Subject: Proposal Attached - Due August 3

Subject: Feedback Needed by May 1

Subject: Client Request for Friday

The worst thing that you can do is put a needed action at the end of a long message. The recipient may not even read what you need until the due date has passed.

## Leave the History When It Matters

When you reply to a message, do not delete the thread unless you are absolutely positive that the reader does not need it.

For example, when you pose a question about a topic in a previous message, your client may need to put your request in context to respond. Going back through previous messages to find information so that a current request makes sense quickly becomes a frustrating waste of time.

One college professor who teaches online said that students sometimes follow up on an old assignment by sending a new message that does not contain the history. Rather than spending time to "recreate history," she requests that they do the legwork by re-sending their question in the previous message that contains the history. Though this approach would not be effective with a business client, it's a good learning opportunity for a student.

At times, an e-mail thread is clutter; at other times, an e-mail thread contains valuable information that provides the context of the current request. Do not start a new thread about an old question; including all needed information shows courtesy.


## Ask Questions to Get a Response

At times, questions are not answered because they are buried in the message or asked in an indirect way.

Speak directly to the reader, and ask a question rather than make a statement, for example:

**Don't Say:**

The conference in Milwaukee is in the planning stages, and it would be helpful for me to know by Friday the participants who will be attending the conference.

**Do Say:**

Who in your department will be attending the conference in Milwaukee? Please let me know by Friday.

By stating your question clearly and concisely, you make it easy for your reader to respond, which shows respect. As a result, you are also are more likely to get your questions answered.

In addition, when you have more than one question, number your questions.

## Keep the Human Element Alive:
### *If You Wouldn't Say It, Don't Write It.*

A computer screen makes it easy to forget that a person with feelings is on the receiving side. As you write a message, keep your thinking tuned into the idea of "dialogue" rather than "monologue."

When you speak with someone, an immediate interchange of ideas occurs, with tone of voice and body language giving important cues. Each person has an opportunity to share and feel listened to. Each person can clarify thinking without going into minute detail. In short, human contact has intangible feedback loops to support communication that technology does not have.

One college professor who teaches nursing students online said, "You wouldn't believe the things that students write in an e-mail that they would never say to my face. When I receive that kind of an e-mail, I call the student. When they find out who is on the line, there's dead silence. Finally I say, 'What did you expect would happen after you sent an e-mail like that to me?'"

When you find yourself writing about a problem rather than its solution, save your draft for later. No one likes being wrong, and no one appreciates feeling blamed. When blame is involved, someone loses face. Losing face is a devastating threat that encourages a defensive response.

When emotions run high, do not even consider e-mail as an option: e-mail is never the medium to convey emotion. Also remember that e-communication can go viral in an instant. Therefore, if you ever find yourself not caring about how the reader will feel or respond, stop writing and wait until you are rested and feel confident.

## Identify the Difference Between Facts and Opinions

Opinions are not facts. Unfortunately, most people do not stop to consider that their opinions result from their own personal interpretations.

Though interpretations are not facts; to some extent, they are options. The messages you give yourself are far more potent than any message you can receive from another. When you assume the worst, you are creating problems for yourself because you are more likely to respond in a negative way.

When opinions run strong, a person is less likely to listen with an open mind. Therefore, when your opinions differ from your client's, e-mail is not an effective way to find common ground. In fact, when you receive a message that you believe is angry or offensive, keep an open mind until you find out more details.

Many issues with e-mail are created because one person interprets a message differently from the way the sender intended. As Lauren, a project manager said, "I'm a Boomer and over the years have received so many angry messages that I don't take any of them personally anymore—I used to, but now I know someone else's anger is not about me—so I just put the message aside until I can respond professionally and then move on."

According to Byron Katie in her book *Loving What Is*, the way to deal with negative thoughts is to challenge them.[3] The next time that you have a negative thought or start telling yourself a negative story, ask yourself, "Is that true?" And then ask again, "Is that really true?"

Most negative thoughts are opinions. If you cannot prove that a negative thought is true, let it go. And even if you can prove that it is true, it's still possible to let it go through a process called forgiveness. Letting go of negative thoughts creates a more peaceful, and sane, state of mind.

As the novelist Anatole France once said, "It is the certainty that they possess the truth that makes men cruel."


## Be Cautious How You CYB (Cover Your Backside)

At times, in the interest in making sure that they have proper documentation, writers copy people who are out of the loop. An example would be copying someone's manager to ensure follow through, which may be necessary at times. However, when supervisors are copied unnecessarily, it sends a subtle message that hampers trust.

An e-mail itself is, in fact, documentation. Copy people outside of the loop only as a last resort. Instead, take other first steps such as sending a follow-up message that states the urgency of the request as well as making a follow-up phone call. The recipient might feel annoyed, but feeling annoyed is better than feeling offended, losing face, or losing trust.

## End Notes

1. Albert, Mehrabian, *Silent Messages*, Wadsworth Publishing Company, 1971.
2. Dona Young, *Eleven Steps to Instantly Improve Your Writing* and *A Guide for Business Writing,* Writer's Toolkit Publishing, 2011.
3. Byron Katie, *Loving What Is: Four Questions That Can Change Your Life*, Three Rivers Press, New York, 2003.

# Part 3

## What about Tone?

Tone is less about what you say and more about how you say it. In fact, tone is also about the way that you interpret, and thus react to, a writer's words.

For example, have you ever thought that a message sounded negative only to change your reaction after you read the message again an hour or day later?

Also consider, do you tend to question someone's tone when you feel good about yourself? Or, are you more likely to question someone's tone when you are having a bad day? When you can, assume the best and let go of the rest.

Tone reflects the emotions of writing and also seeps out through **micro-messages:** *the messages hidden between the lines*. At times, the unspoken micro-message has more impact on tone than the spoken message.

### Keep a Positive Focus

To stay positive, focus on what will go right if procedures are followed rather than on what will go wrong if they are not.

A human reaction to being told *no* is to show *resistance*; resistance is part of everyone's emotional makeup. Because resistance can be unconscious, a person does not have complete control over it. In fact, the best way to control resistance is to avoid creating situations that bring it to life.

For example, even good things can sound threatening if stated in a negative way:

**Negative:**

You can't return this item because you don't have the receipt.

**Positive:**

To give you a refund, I must have the receipt.

**Negative:**

You can't take time off until you complete the project.

**Positive:**

Once you complete the project, you can take a few days off.

**Negative:**

You cannot work with this client on your own.

**Positive:**

You should consider taking a team approach with this client.

**Negative:**

When you are late, you disrupt the entire meeting.

**Positive:**

When everyone arrives on time, our meetings run smoothly.

Everyone appreciates positive words—even subtle, affirmative comments add positive energy. As Mother Theresa once said, "Kind words can be short and easy to speak, but their echoes are truly endless."

## Avoid Trigger Words

Some words trigger negative reactions. For example, when some people hear the word *policy*, they feel as if a door is being slammed in their face. In fact, the word *policy* can even have legal connotations. Possible substitutes are *procedures* and *processes*.

**Don't Say:**

It's our policy that all paperwork must be completed and received before any changes are made to an account.

An alternative would be to state what the policy is without using the word *policy*.

**Do Say:**

As soon as we receive your paperwork, we will make all necessary changes in your account.

Some other words that trigger a negative emotional response are *unsatisfactory, unacceptable, unfair, not, never . . . had enough? Never again . . . .*

Here's the bottom line: your goal is for your client to listen with an open mind until you can work through to a win-win solution. Negative trigger words create a divide and close the mind to options.

## Connect Through the "You" Viewpoint

Do you tend to start a lot of your sentences with the personal pronoun *I*? If so, you are keeping the focus on yourself, rather than the reader.

By speaking directly to your reader through the "you" viewpoint, you engage your reader directly and tune in to your reader's needs more effectively; for example:

**"I" Viewpoint:**

*I* am writing to let you know that *I* would like to invite you to our next meeting.

**"You" Viewpoint:**

*You* are invited to attend our next meeting, or

Would *you* be interested in attending our next meeting?

By using the "you" viewpoint, you cue the reader how to respond, for example:

**"I" Viewpoint**:

*I* would like to know more information about the new policy.

**"You" Viewpoint:**

(*You*) Please tell me about the new policy.

**"I" Viewpoint**:

*I* would like to know what you think about the situation.

**"You" Viewpoint:**

What do *you* think about the situation?

By putting the focus on your reader, the "you" viewpoint also improves the tone of your document.

**"I" Viewpoint:**

*I* appreciate the job you did on the proposal.

**"You" Viewpoint:**

*You* did a great job on the proposal.

Though the "you" viewpoint helps readers stay connected, the "I" viewpoint is effective and even necessary at times; so do not try to eliminate every sentence that begins with *I*.

In addition, when you are dealing with conflict, use "I" statements so that you can discuss your feelings without sounding accusatory.

## Express Your Feelings with "I" Statements

At times, expressing negative feelings is a necessity. One way to express your point of view without raising the defenses of the other person is to use "I" statements.

An "I" statement is more than a sentence that begins with "I"; an "I" statement is actually a sequence of three statements, for example:

Part 1: How do you feel?

Part 2: Why?

Part 3: Because?

Use "I" statements to express yourself verbally; if a situation is serious enough to merit "I" statements, e-mail is not the correct medium.

**Example 1:**

| | |
|---|---|
| Part 1: How do you feel? | I feel frustrated |
| Part 2: Why? | when I receive angry messages, and |
| Part 3: Because? | I don't know how to respond. |

Be careful not to turn the "I" statement into a camouflaged "you" statement.

**For example:**

I feel frustrated when *you* send me angry messages.

The goal is to keep the attention on the behavior and your feelings, and not the person doing it.

**Example 2:**

| | |
|---|---|
| Part 1: How do you feel? | I feel discouraged and unfocused |
| Part 2: Why? | when I am yelled at, and |
| Part 3: Because? | I'm not able to work effectively. |

By speaking about your own feelings, you are less likely to tap into another person's defenses and more likely to ensure that the other person listens to what you are saying. Also, by speaking from your own point of view, you are less likely to receive an argumentative response.

People can argue about what seem to be accusations against them, but they cannot legitimately argue with you about your feelings.

By working on "I" statements, you can also tune in to your own feelings more clearly. By having the courage to share "I" statements in important relationships, you work toward bringing the relationship to a higher level of understanding and integrity.

## Use the Tactful Voice to Avoid Pointing Blame

The two voices of writing are the *active voice* and the *passive voice*. The *passive voice* is considered the tactful voice because a passive sentence does not need a subject that performs  the action of its verb: the passive voice allows you to focus on the problem and not the person.

The passive voice is perfect for situations that have the potential to involve blame, for example:

**Active:**
You made a mistake on the August invoice.

**Passive**:
A mistake was made on the August invoice.

**Active:**
You did not inform George that the incident was not reported.

**Passive:**
George was not informed that the incident was not reported.

**Active:**
Bob did not consult the client about the change in her account.

**Passive:**
The client was not consulted about the change in her account.

Whenever you are speaking about an error, the tone sounds less accusatory by not pointing a finger. Not holding someone accountable is an important quality at times.

If you use the passive voice when you give constructive feedback, the listener is more likely to take in the message objectively.

## Turn Negative Feedback into Constructive Feedback

The goal of feedback is to change behavior, not to hurt the person receiving it.

However, just as receiving feedback can be difficult, giving someone feedback on change or growth issues can also be difficult.

When you give someone feedback, focus on the distinction between *negative feedback* and *constructive feedback*.

- *Negative feedback* identifies the problem but not the solution.
- *Constructive feedback* identifies the problem, offers a possible solution, and opens a dialog.

Constructive feedback doesn't point an accusing finger at an offender; it gets the involved persons talking. However, when feedback is conveyed ineffectively, the person receiving it can feel attacked. To help ensure that your motives are in the right place, before you give any kind of negative feedback, ask yourself the following: *What is my purpose in giving this feedback? What do I want to achieve?*

The way feedback is given (and received) can enhance or destroy a relationship as well as an individual's career at a specific place of employment. If you have any doubts about how to convey constructive feedback, role play the situation with a peer or your manager.

The best time to address inappropriate behavior is soon after the behavior occurred. However, constructive feedback must also be given at a time when neither the speaker nor the listener feels emotional about it. For example, if either party is upset, that is not the time to address the behavior or incident: the speaker will not be objective and constructive, the listener will not hear the important points, and the response may be defensive rather than responsible.

When people feel emotional, call a time out until things settle down and an objective discussion can occur.

## Give PCS Feedback: Positive – Constructive – Supportive

Honest feedback leading to growth can be difficult to hear, but feedback can also be difficult to give. When you give constructive feedback:

1. Start with an honest, *positive* statement,

2. State the *constructive* feedback, and finally,

3. End on a *supportive* note; for example:

> Margaret,
>
> Your reports are thorough and accurate, which I appreciate.
>
> However, your last two reports have not been received on time. Will you be able to meet next month's deadline?
>
> Do you need additional support?
>
> Isabelle

By starting out with a positive comment, the recipient is more likely to listen receptively. Using questions also keeps the discussion open so that you can get at core issues.

When addressing a serious issue, meet in person and in private. Also, if you need to document concerns, wait until after you have spoken: you may clarify misunderstandings as you discuss the issues together.

By putting information in writing after your discussion, you have documentation; but more important, your summary helps ensure that you both have the same understanding.

Here's an example of a possible follow-up message:

> Margaret,
>
> As we discussed, here is the process you will follow for your monthly reports:
>
> 1. When you do not receive data from other departments on time, you will follow up with department managers.
> 2. If your report still cannot be completed on time, you will let me know in advance and give me the details.
>
> Please let me know if you need additional support.
>
> Isabelle

Depending on the circumstances, you may also want to write in the passive voice and use "I" statements.

By following a pattern of comments that are *positive*, then *constructive*, and finally *supportive*, you are giving the other person the benefit of the doubt. Everyone appreciates support and deserves at least one second chance.

## Use the Indirect Message Style for Bad News

Once in a while, everyone needs to convey news the reader does not expect or would prefer not receiving. A *bad news message* is one of the few times when an indirect message achieves better results than a direct message.

In an indirect message, include details before stating outcomes or conclusions. By explaining the logic and background details first, you give the reader an opportunity to understand the *why* of the unwelcome decision, for example:

**Message 1, Giving bad news using an *indirect* style:**

Charley,

Here's information about your request.

I checked with corporate, and they said they were already over budget for this summer's conference. However, they thought your suggestion to plan in a team-building workshop was excellent, and they will put that on the priority list for next year.

In the meantime, can you find another solution? Let me know what you think.

Best regards,

John

---

Notice the difference in tone between the preceding message and the following one. *Does the way the information is structured affect the tone?*

**Message 2, Giving bad news using a *direct* style:**

Charley,

Your request for a team-building workshop has been denied.

I checked with corporate, and they said they were already over budget for this summer's conference. However, they thought your suggestion to plan in a team-building workshop was excellent, and they will put that on the priority list for next year.

John

When bad news is presented first, the reader is likely to have an immediate negative reaction, which colors the remainder of the message. In fact, the reader may not even bother to read the rest of the message.

In the introduction, state the purpose in a general way. Then give enough explanation so that the rationale leading to the news makes sense. State your main point or bad news toward the end of the body or possibly in the conclusion.

In the closing paragraph, let your reader know that he or she may contact you for additional information.

## Keep it Simple

When you receive a message that triggers a negative response, the best thing that you can do is to process the message until you can simplify your response.

Take a look at the e-mail below in which the writer is responding with a trigger reaction. *How do you feel as you read it?* Before looking at the next page, consider how to revise the message below to get a better result.

---

John,

I received your message suggesting that we cut this fall's sales meetings by one day. I know you're not going to be pleased with my reaction, but I'm already feeling stressed out trying to fit in everything that I have planned with my staff. In fact, they are all enthused about the meetings and getting prepared for them. It would be a major letdown for me to have to tell them that we now have to cut 20 percent of everything that we have planned.

So if you go forward with this idea, don't expect me to support it. Sure, it's a good idea to cut the budget, but this isn't the road to take.

Charley

---

By focusing only on areas of agreement, here's how Charley might have responded:

> John,
>
> Cutting the budget is a great idea—when do you have time to discuss this?
>
> Hope your day goes well.
>
> Charley

If negative trigger words create a divide and close the mind to options, negative trigger responses can lead to even worse results.

When you are caught off guard, don't respond until you can clarify your thinking and find common ground. Everyone faces compromises—give yourself time to process information until you find a genuine solution.

The following quote by John Dewey demonstrates why thinking "outside of the box" is such an uncommon and difficult achievement:

> One can think reflectively only when one is willing to endure suspense and to undergo the trouble of searching. To many persons both suspense of judgment and intellectual search are disagreeable; they want to get them ended as soon as possible. They cultivate an over-positive and dogmatic habit of mind, or feel perhaps that a condition of doubt will be regarded as evidence of mental inferiority. . . . To be genuinely thoughtful, we must be willing to sustain and protract that state of doubt which is the stimulus to thorough inquiry . . . .[1]

## Complain Effectively:

## Be Positive and Seek a Win-Win Solution

Making a complaint is an unpleasant experience that can also feel emotional. Agreements have been broken or expectations have been violated, and you may have experienced some harm, financial or otherwise. When you have a complaint, putting your complaint in writing will help you clarify the situation, document it, and get results.

In fact, when you take the time to complain in writing, you are actually doing a favor for the ones to whom you are complaining: you are giving them an opportunity to right a wrong. You are also giving insight into a problem that can then be corrected before others experience your pain and inconvenience.

When you complain, you will get better results by start-ing with positive information, such as the fact that you are a valued client. In fact, it's to your advantage to write your complaint assuming that the issue will be rectified. By doing so, you set a tone that benefits both you and the recipient.

In fact, many people make the mistake of pointing their complaint directly at a customer service representative who has had absolutely nothing to do with creating the problem. By realizing that a customer service representative may have some leeway to shift the policy to your advantage, you are more likely to state your issue objectively.

Of course, when you write your draft, you are likely to vent. That's why editing is a critical element of the writing process; and a critical element of editing is time and space: leave enough time between your first draft and your final edit so that you are confident and objective before you click *send*.

Any effective complaint will aid the receiver in saving face and in doing something to solve the problem. Therefore, end your complaint with a suggestion in how to turn the situation into a *win-win solution*. Anything less, and you are just blowing off steam and reducing the likelihood that you will get what you want.

## Respect the Gatekeepers

Unfortunately, some people change their tone based on the level of employee to whom they are speaking.

In fact, one customer service agent said that when some callers can't get what they want, they become rude and ask to speak with a manager or someone in higher authority. As soon as the caller gets someone on the line who they think is a manager, the person's tone changes. The point here is that asking to speak to a manager is appropriate at times, but being rude is never appropriate and always unnecessary.

Another example comes from Pat, an administrative assistant who shared that the only people who get through to her boss are the ones who treat her with respect. She said with a smile that most people don't understand the power structure: people who are low on the totem pole control important resources, such as the schedule and attention of the people in power. Before meeting anyone new, her boss asks her for her initial perceptions.

By nurturing the relationship with the gatekeeper, you are creating an important ally.

End Note

1.  John Dewey, *How We Think*, D. C. Health and Company, Massachusetts, 1933.

# Part 4

## What Are the Facts and Best Practices?

Best practices for e-mail establish a pivot point from which to make effective decisions. These guidelines define expectations and develop boundaries so that decisions become easier to make.

Since processing feedback is an element of angry e-mail, guidelines for receiving feedback are also included here.

### E-Mail Facts

Over time, you might feel as if your co-workers have become like family and that you are a permanent part of your company. That is not the case, so do not let those cozy feelings lead you to letting your guard down, even if your father owns the company—here's why:

- E-mail messages are official documents and can be used in litigation.

Always remain aware that your messages can become evidence in legal actions. As a result, your e-mail can also become part of the public domain. As the former employees of Enron discovered, even casual messages to friends can become part of the litigation process.

- Your computer at work is the company's property.

Whether you are aware of it or not, your company can—and probably does—monitor your use of e-mail. Companies have the legal right to review any messages that you send or receive. In fact, you have no legal right to privacy for any type of Internet usage while at work, even if you are using a personal e-mail account.

- Once you click *send*, your message is out of your control forever.

Even deleted messages do not go away and can be restored by experts when the need arises. In addition, anyone can forward your message to the CEO of your corporation or a public site. In other words, any e-mail that you send can go around the world; and you can't stop it, even if you know about it. Like any sort of communication, your message can be twisted and read out of context. And just about anything can go viral in a heartbeat.

We live in a time in which people suddenly find themselves scrutinized by the entire world. Most people who find themselves immersed in notoriety do not expect it to happen . . . until after it has suddenly happened. Then life feels unbearably out of control.

To avoid heartbreaking scenarios, use all forms of electronic communication appropriately. Do not say or do anything that you would not mind having discussed on the national evening news or a morning talk show, and you will be safe.

## Best Practices for E-Mail

E-mail does not have rigid rules as compared other types of business correspondence, such as business letters. Though e-mail usage continues to evolve, use the following guidelines to keep communications flowing on a professional level:

1. Start your message with the most important information: put purpose up front and clearly state what you need from the reader at the *beginning* of the message.

2. Respond to e-mail within one or two days, even if you are simply acknowledging that you are working on the request.

3. Wait about two days after you send a message to follow up on an unmet request or make a phone call.

4. Use an automatic out-of-office response if you will be out of reach for a day or more.

5. Do not Cc people unless they are in the loop. When people are copied unnecessarily, it wastes their time and can send a negative message that creates an awkward situation.

6. Press "reply all" *only* when you are sure that everyone needs to receive your message; when only the sender needs a reply, other recipients become annoyed because it wastes their time.

7. Include a note at the top of a group message that you send stating that only you should receive a reply. Consider developing group lists in which you show the names but not the e-mail addresses of recipients.

8. Forward messages rather than use Bcc when you want to keep people in the loop; this keeps the communication above board.

9. Use standard capitalization: all CAPS connote shouting; use all lower case only if you are a techie writing to other techies—otherwise, adapt your writing for your audience.

10. Never use text abbreviations in e-mail: *When in doubt, spell it out.* (When you send a message from a mobile device, include a reference such as "Sent from my Blackberry" so your reader does not expect perfection or even a detailed response.)

11. Use an accurate and updated subject line so that your reader can refer to your message and file it easily; include action needed in the subject line.

12. Avoid using *read now* and *urgent*; all messages are urgent; demonstrate urgency by using a subject line that includes action needed and a due date.

13. Avoid sending the following types of information via e-mail: confidential, sensitive, or bad news.

14. Encrypt sensitive information such as credit card numbers. (If you don't know how to encrypt information, do a search on "sending sensitive information by e-mail.")

15. Use an *indirect message style* when you must send bad news; however, consider other options before using e-mail.

16. Use visual persuasion so that your reader can pick up key points at a glance; for example, use white space, side headings, bolding, and numbering to enhance your message.

17. Number questions and requests so that they stand out.

18. Add a note at the beginning of forwarded messages: explain the action that the reader should take, or let the reader know that the message is only *FYI* (for your information).

19. Leave the history unless you are certain the reader does not need it; deleted history can create frustration and lost time for your reader.

20. Avoid jargon; however, if you use an acronym or initialism, spell it out the first time, putting the abbreviated form in parentheses: "Include your employee identification number (EID)." Or you can use a less traditional approach, flipping the order: "Include your EID (employee identification number)."

21. Avoid slang, and do not use sarcasm; refrain from sending jokes or being humorous, and use emoticons rarely, if at all.

22. Use e-mail sparingly for personal messages, even if your company allows it.

23. Avoid sounding suspicious, as in "Delete this message upon reading."

24. Avoid saying, "No, that's not our policy," and instead state what you *can do* for a client.

25. Do not respond to controversial or emotional messages unless you are confident and objective; better yet, call the person.

Since part of dealing with angry e-mail involves receiving negative feedback, let's look at how to respond to negative feedback.

## Guidelines for Receiving Feedback

Feedback is a part of everyone's career; in fact, if you look closely, you might see that it is also a part of most people's daily lives. However, even constructive feedback can catch a person off guard. And no one likes to be publicly accused of making mistakes.

Most human beings find it difficult to accept their own mistakes. Giving the other guy a break seems easier than being kind and gentle with oneself. *Why is that?* Part of the reason may relate to overly-high expectations.

Do you expect yourself to be perfect, becoming frustrated when you are not? Do you expect yourself to know all the answers? When you make a mistake, do you replay it over and again in your head, beating yourself up over it?

Handled effectively, negative feedback can lead to significant growth. As R. G. Ingersoll once said, "The greatest test of courage on the earth is to bear defeat without losing heart." Since negative feedback often feels defeating, let's examine how to receive it professionally.

- First, *thank the person* for taking the time to point out the behavior. Whether or not you agree with the feedback is not the immediate issue.

- *Refrain from arguing* and do not immediately discount the feedback (even if you do not agree with it at that moment).

- *Clarify the information.* At times, the message that a person receives is not the same as the message the sender intended.

- *Ask questions* so that you get specific details, especially if the feedback feels vague or general.

- *Reflect* on the comments and try to understand how your actions could have led to the other person's perceptions.

After you have had time to think, consider the following:

- *If the feedback is accurate*, accept responsibility and avoid placing blame on others. If appropriate, apologize.

- *If you can refrain from being defensive*, offer an explanation (but not an excuse). Do not try to *convince* the other person you were justified in your actions; after you offer your explanation, leave it up to the listener to come to his or her own conclusions.

- *If you feel the feedback is not accurate*, you may want to wait longer or seek input before you respond. In the meantime, you can say something such as, "Thank you for your feedback. Before I respond, I need to think about it. If you don't mind, I'll follow up with you later today or tomorrow."

When you receive constructive feedback, you will achieve the best result by defining how to solve the problem. Put the feedback in perspective: receiving honest, constructive feedback does not mean that you have failed, but it might mean that you need to make changes or get additional training. The hardest thing to change is a way of thinking; but at times, it is necessary and even liberating.

When you receive constructive feedback, don't act on it immediately:

- Reflect on the experience, and put it in perspective.
- Journal about it; analyze your behavior and what you could do differently.
- Get a good night's rest before you make any important decisions.

*When a situation is emotionally charged, avoid responding in writing.* Whatever you put in writing can follow you throughout your career at a corporation. (In fact, now that the world is online, what you send electronically can follow you the rest of your life.) Once you feel calm, rested, and objective, meet with the person face to face, if possible.

The key to turning the situation around is responding appropriately. Unfortunately, many people make a situation or relationship worse by the way they respond. Keep in mind that all feedback, when dealt with constructively, can be the turning point for positive results. And you will feel different once you've had a chance to process the information and get some rest.

Worse than negative feedback is when people withhold accurate feedback that could lead to growth. When people withhold constructive feedback, it does not mean that a situation is all right; the situation will continue to worsen as long as the problem persists.

*Mistakes are a vital part of learning.* Mistakes are also a price of being human, and no one is immune. Doing any job effectively involves continual adjustments and constant learning. By accepting mistakes gracefully and learning from them, you set yourself apart from others.

# Part 5

## What's Your Plan?

Each time that you become angry, think of your anger as a *learning moment*: resolving anger is a process issue not an outcome.

Has something happened to open an old wound? Ask yourself, "Why am I feeling so intense about this?" Try to see all of the ingredients, piece by piece. By understanding the deeper roots of anger, you are more equipped to deal with the superficial wounds that angry e-mail and other types of feedback may cause.

Also remember that your feelings result from the messages that you give yourself, not from what others say or do. How you interpret the situation determines how you will respond. Thus, when you receive a message that makes you feel angry or hurt, do some soul searching and then develop your strategy:

1. Have you effectively defined the problem?
2. Have you defined your objectives?
3. Have you identified common ground?
4. Have you developed your options and assessed them?

As you implement your next steps, remember to:

- Give others the benefit of the doubt.
- Focus on the mission, not the issues.

- Focus on the solution, not the problem.
- Seek areas of agreement.
- Separate personal feelings from business relationships.
- Ensure that your communications do not include blame.
- Give the answer, don't tell the story.
- Screen your response for micro-messages.
- Understand and respect diversity.
- Phone, rather than send an e-mail, when you have concerns.
- Do not write it if you would not say it to someone face to face.
- Accept feedback gracefully.
- Apologize when the situation calls for it.

Always remember the human elements of communication, which involve feelings, passions, fears, and insecurities as well as forgiveness and appreciation. No one is perfect, which means that everyone makes mistakes. By giving others leeway, they are more likely to bestow that grace upon you when you fall short.

At times, a human voice can melt barriers that written words cannot, and an apology can release the emotions of hurt feelings that may be lurking beneath the surface. Once trust is violated, relationships become challenging. By screening sensitive messages for clarity and tone, you help ensure that you are not inadvertently sending a negative micro-message.

By keeping your focus on the prize, you are more likely to write a professional message for which you will not feel guilty or for which you will not experience reprisal. And what's the prize? Your sense of confidence, your reputation, and the trust you enhance among clients and colleagues. Because let's face it, as soon as someone receives an angry e-mail, others know about it.

So let's end where we began with a reminder that it's your relationships that support you in getting your job done—not simply the exchange of information through messages.

And if all else fails, remember this:

*Success is the best revenge.*

# About the Author

Dona Young is a teacher, facilitator, and writing coach who believes that writing is a powerful learning tool that shapes our lives and careers.

For more information about Young's workshops on effective business writing, go to **www.youngcommunication.com**.

Young has an M.A. from The University of Chicago and is the author of the following professional writing books:

*Eleven Steps to Instantly Improve Your Writing*

*Business Communication and Writing:*
*Enhancing Career Flexibility*

*A Guide for Business Writing*

*The Writer's Handbook: Grammar for Writing*

*The Mechanics of Writing*

*Business English: Writing for the Global Workplace*

*Foundations of Business Communication:*
*An Integrative Approach*

*Writing Effective E-Mail in Conflict Situations, the Workbook*


And on the lighter side:

*The Princess and Her Gift:*
*A Tale on the Practical Magic of Learning*

*The Little Prince Who Taught a Village to Sing*

www.youngcommunication.com

65